VANESSA BATES is an award-winning playwright for stage and radio and also writes for film and television. Her plays include *Trailer*, *Light Begins to Fade*, *Every Second*, *The Magic Hour*, *PORN.CAKE*, *Checklist for an Armed Robber*, *Chipper* and *Darling Oscar*. She adapted *A Ghost in My Suitcase* for Barking Gecko Theatre, Melbourne International Arts Festival 2018, Sydney Festival 2019 and Perth Festival 2019. Her plays have been produced by the Sydney Theatre Company, Malthouse Theatre, Belvoir B-Sharp, Griffin, Vitalstatistix, Ensemble Theatre, atyp and Tantrum Theatre, among others. Her work has won a NSW Premier's Literary Award, AWGIE Award, Inscription Chairman's Award and Inscription New Work Award and has been shortlisted for the Victorian Premier's New Play Award, Griffin Award and STC Patrick White Playwrights Award.

*Yilin Kong as Ting Ting in Barking Gecko's production in 2018. (Photo: Stefan Gosatti)*

# A Ghost in my Suitcase

Adapted by Vanessa Bates

From the novel by Gabrielle Wang

**CURRENCY PRESS**
The performing arts publisher

CURRENCY PLAYS

First published in 2019
by Currency Press Pty Ltd,
Gadigal Land, Suite 310, 46–56 Kippax Street, Surry Hills, NSW 2010, Australia.
enquiries@currency.com.au
www.currency.com.au

Reprinted 2022, 2024.



*A Ghost in My Suitcase* by Gabrielle Wang (the novel) first published by Penguin Group (Australia) 2009.



Typeset by Dean Nottle for Currency Press.
Printed by CanPrint Communications, ACT.
Cover design by Emma Bennetts.

Currency Press acknowledges the Traditional Owners of the Country on which we live and work. We pay our respects to all Aboriginal and Torres Strait Islander Elders, past and present.

A catalogue record for this book is available from the National Library of Australia

# Contents

*Amanda Ma (left) as Por Por and Alice Keohavong as Celeste in Barking Gecko's production in 2018. (Photo: Stefan Gosatti)*

# MAKING SPACE FOR SPIRITS

As the child of a librarian, I grew up devouring fantasy books, my spare hours spent lost in strange worlds. So when I stumbled across Gabrielle Wang's wonderful novel *A Ghost in My Suitcase*, while searching for new stories for Barking Gecko Theatre Company, I was beyond excited. Here was an Australian fantasy epic with all the delicate moral questioning and fierce imagination of Philip Pullman or Ursula Le Guin. And although the story was set entirely in China and full of the fantastical, it was quintessentially Australian in its exploration of diaspora and belonging. Almost everyone living in Australia has roots elsewhere. Many of us feel the pull of this history very strongly and I felt this aspect would resonate strongly with children, as they develop their sense of place and identity in the world. I still feel so fortunate to have been able to work with the formidably talented Vanessa Bates and the entire creative team to find a new form for this story and share it with thousands of children around the country.

We began the adaptation process with hundreds of pages full of wonderful words. And some big creative challenges! The novel is a great yarn spun by a master storyteller, with many layers. The most obvious layer is the action-adventure story, which carries us along with a series of escalating ghost battles in an ancient Chinese water town. Then there is the layer of revelation—family secrets are gradually uncovered as we travel onwards and the past and present draw closer together. And beneath these is a layer of reflection—the deep interiority of the central character Celeste who is learning to process her grief, guided by the calm Daoist philosophy of her grandmother. In adapting the novel to the stage, the challenge was how to make these layers work in a theatrical form. And we found a key answer in the idea of 'negative space'.

> 'The Uses of Not'
> Thirty spokes meet in the hub.
> Where the wheel isn't is where it's useful.
> Hollowed out, clay makes a pot.

Where the pot's not is where it's useful.
Cut doors and windows to make a room.
Where the room isn't, there's room for you.
So the profit in what is is in the use of what isn't.

Lao Tzu,
from *Tao Te Ching*,
translated by Ursula Le Guin

Negative space is something that Daoist poet-philosopher Lao Tzu understood 2,500 years ago. In fact, he explains it so well that I am tempted to just leave it at that. But I have been asked to write a few more words, so for those who are interested, I'll use the space to explore how we applied this idea to Vanessa's adaptation and our production.

Negative space is not always easy to define in the theatre, but I like to think of it as space left intentionally empty for an audience to fill. This is vital if an audience is to be truly engaged. When and how to use negative space is a big question, particularly when adapting a multi-layered work of fantasy such as this one. There are times to lean into the literal depiction of spectacle and fantastical imagery and times to leave space free for the imagination of the audience. In some ways I think that for Vanessa, translating the book into theatrical form with space for an audience to feel and respond, was as much an act of creation of something new as one of adaptation of an existing work.

Our process has been one of paring back words, actions, scenes and characters to make room. For theatre creatures who love the English language as much as Vanessa and I do, this has been about discovering new languages—in light, sound, tempo and architecture. It has taken three years of disciplined subtraction. In this time, we have had the great luxury of four creative developments including two trips to China and a trial season, followed by performances at three national festivals. At each stage, the 'pot' has hollowed a little more until, by our final season in Perth (this published script), I feel that we made enough room for audience and actors.

As you would imagine for a work of fantasy, there are elements of our production where the lyrical language of the novel gives way to pure visual spectacle. This applied most strongly to the action layer in the story: a kabuki drop where a silky fabric descends from the heavens as night falls over a haunted house, cloaking the stage in darkness; or a highly detailed filmed 'tracking shot' down the canal of a water town, projected on every vertical surface in the space; or the cacophony of real-world images that is Shanghai airport, or the climactic martial-arts-style battle with two ghosts. Little needs to be said when you are showing so much visually.

Then there were scenes where very little was shown either. One of our young test audience's favourite scenes was our depiction of a bus full of frogs, created primarily with the artful composition of actors' bodies and sound. Here the audience are enlisted to create the image with their own imaginative forces—the frogs, the bus and the world of rural China beyond the foggy windows. Or for our first ghost encounter, the ghost of the French chef, who never appears on stage but whose earthquake-like energy manifests in actors' bodies and in sound.

Negative space also exists in Vanessa's text itself: language constructed in a way that invites reflection via omissions, inferences, ambiguity and mystery. Celeste asks, 'Por Por, why do people have to die?', which is answered with silence and a brief wordless touch between the actors. Most of the 'interior' passages—Celeste's asides to the audience—have gradually lost almost all of their text, as we realised the actor and dramatic context communicate so much more powerfully with silence.

'Begin as you mean to continue' is a useful maxim in art as well as in life. So a big question in adapting *A Ghost in My Suitcase* was: who has a seat at the table in the very first development? When our creative team first met in early 2016, there were five of us. Vanessa and I led the process of dissection of the novel—labelling its bones, muscles and arteries in a process vital to give our adaptation its physiology. But other aspects of our time together shaped our approach on a deeper level. My co-director Ching Ching Ho brought a wealth of unique perspectives, provocations and cultural insights into the room. Designer Zoe Atkinson inspired us to think in multiple theatrical languages and distil the work to theme and image. And novelist Gabi Wang taught us Tai Chi and read to us from Ursula Le Guin's stunning translation of Lao Tzu.

These first offers set the tone for all that was to come over the following three years—the wise Daoist aphorisms of Por Por, the fluid ghost-fighting style of Ting Ting, the constantly shifting set of overlapping boxes and the moments of nuanced cultural exchange in the characters' interactions all have their origins in this beginning. The show continued to evolve in this spirit up until our final season, with investigations of design and use of space given equal weight to explorations of text and the body of the actor.

In the following months, media artist Sohan Ariel Hayes came on board to collect and select imagery for the show, including travelling with Ching Ching on a field trip to locations around China. The sound design was lovingly crafted by Perth composer Rachael Dease, featuring her hauntingly beautiful compositions which brought Celeste's ghost songs to life. Matt Marshall effortlessly sculpted light to give each ghost its own unique energy and ambiance. And among all this, we had multiple rounds of nationwide casting over two years to find five extraordinary, muli-talented performers: Amanda Ma, Frieda Lee, Yilin Kong, Imanuel Dado and Alice Keohavong.

So on to the only question that really matters: what have audiences made of it? Children around the country have responded with joy and a depth of feeling. The best responses have been wordless—the numerous recreations of ghost fights in foyers around the country after each show, as the children attempt to replicate Yilin Kong's martial arts moves. Consistently children have said their favourite moment in the show is not a ghost battle, it is the moment where Celeste finally scatters her mother's ashes and finds release. I have loved the letters we have received. From the child who wrote us a poem about his newfound love for kabuki drops, to the one who said the play 'made me feel completely void from reality', to the child who told us 'It was my first time attending the theatre … it made me feel like I was in China'. I'll share one adult response, which speaks to the cultural meaning that an audience can find in stories like this one:

> Tonight Mum and I were entranced by a story that was about us. I was struck by the feeling of wanting to cry simultaneously while I was beaming from ear to ear. Experiencing your difference as an identity is powerful … As a child of mixed race in Australia, at times I felt, or was made to feel, like my identity was nothing. To see Celeste's strength as a Eurasian woman was stunning. Representation matters, matters, matters … Thank you to the mighty little team at Barking Gecko Theatre for sharing this beautiful production.

Finally, the process of inspiration can travel in unexpected directions. After our first development, novelist Gabrielle Wang began work on a sequel, which she's called *Ting Ting the Ghosthunter*. The novel acknowledges that first group of creatives that met in the Melbourne Arts Centre way back at the start of 2016:

> A special thank you to Matt, Felix [Ching Ching], Vanessa and Zoe—fellow ghost travellers and play makers.

It is a deeply satisfying thought to feel that we have somehow contributed to Gabi's next novel (a great read by the way!).

Thank you again to Vanessa Bates and the entire creative team for all their passion and craft in adapting this work for the stage. And a huge thank you to Barking Gecko and to Perth, Sydney and Melbourne Festivals for investing in the work's creation. With a published script, I hope there are many more young people who see, read and perform the work and make their own connections! I look forward to future teams of ghost hunters taking the story somewhere none of us expect in its next incarnations.

*Matt Edgerton*
*July 2019*

Matt Edgerton is a theatre director. He helped develop *A Ghost in My Suitcase* during his time as Artistic Director of Barking Gecko Theatre Company.

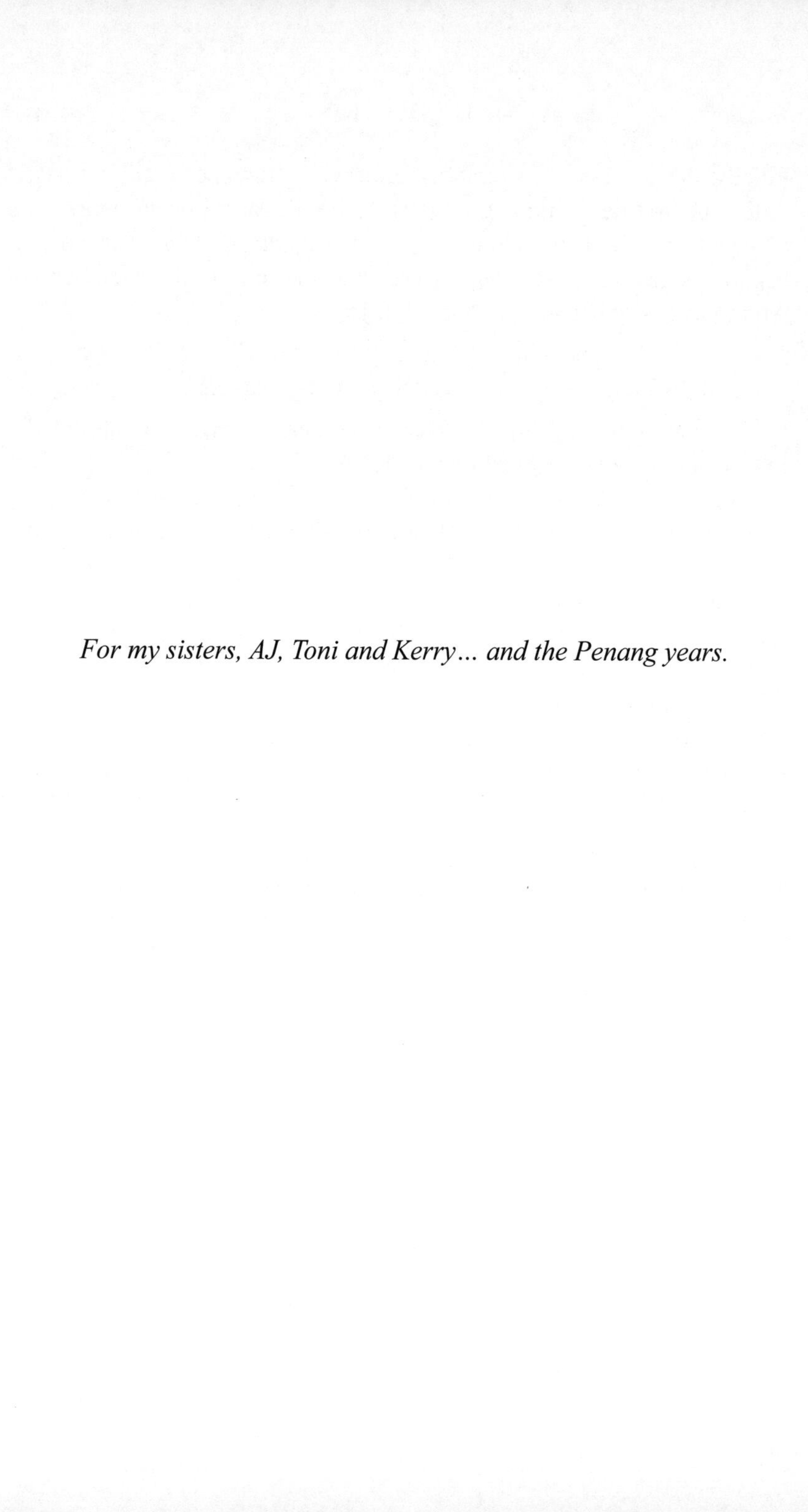

*For my sisters, AJ, Toni and Kerry... and the Penang years.*

*A Ghost in My Suitcase* was first produced by Barking Gecko Theatre on 18 October 2018 at the Arts Centre, Melbourne, with the following cast:

| | |
|---|---|
| CELESTE | Alice Keohavong |
| POR POR | Amanda Ma |
| TING TING | Yilin Kong |
| FEMALE ENSEMBLE | Frieda Lee |
| MALE ENSEMBLE | Imanuel Dado |

Directors, Ching Ching Ho and Matt Edgerton
Set and Costume Designer, Zoë Atkinson
Lighting Designer, Matthew Marshall
Composer and Sound Designer, Rachael Dease
Media Artist, Sohan Ariel Hayes
Fight Director, Andy Fraser
Puppetry Consultant, Michael Barlow

## CHARACTERS

CELESTE

POR POR

TING TING

AIR HOSTESS

LING FENG

MRS WANG

MR GUO

MRS TAN

FAT BELLY GHOST

BOATMAN

SHEN DA PAI (1 AND 2)

Also various non-speaking characters

Adapted from the novel *A Ghost in My Suitcase* by Gabrielle Wang

*1. THE BEGINNING*

CELESTE *appears, walking slowly towards the audience.*

*Images appear from her dream: water rippling, a giant fish. All are projected on a screen behind her. We hear a fragment of folk song.*

CELESTE: Mama? Mama? Mama?

*The indistinct shape of* MAMA *appears momentarily from within the dream and then disappears again.*

Mama, I'm here!

*Lights as* CELESTE *holds a wrapped wooden box of her mother's ashes.*

[*To the audience*] Each night I try to dream of Mama. I never quite see her. Instead, I see … a sleeping moon, a giant fish, a stream of water, rippling. And I hear … a song I can't quite recognise, the flow of its melody carrying me along …

*She unwraps the wooden box.*

*Behind* CELESTE, *projection transforms the large 'mother box' into a giant version of this box of ashes.*

[*To the audience*] Mama always wanted to return to China. So, I'm bringing her ashes back. Back to the home of our ancestors.

*The voice of an* AIR HOSTESS *is heard, during which* CELESTE *puts the box carefully away in her backpack. We see projections of Shanghai airport.*

AIR HOSTESS: [*voiceover, in Mandarin*]
女士们，先生们：飞机正在下降。请您回原位坐好，系好安全带，收起小桌板，将座椅靠背调整到正常位置。所有个人电脑及电子设备必须处于关闭状态。请你确认您的手提物品是否已妥善安放。稍后，我们将调暗客舱灯光。谢谢！
[*Nǚshìmen, xiānshēngmen: Fēijī zhèngzài xiàjiàng. Qǐng nín huí yuán wèi zuò hǎo, xì hǎo ānquán dài, shōu qǐ xiǎo zhuō bǎn, jiāng zuò yǐ kàobèi tiáozhěng dào zhèngcháng wèizhì. Suǒyǒu gèrén diànnǎo jí diànzǐ shèbèi bìxū chǔyú guānbì zhuàngtài. Qǐng nǐ quèrèn nín de*

*shǒutí wùpǐn shìfǒu yǐ tuǒshàn ānfàng. Shāo hòu, wǒmen jiāng diào àn kècāng dēngguāng. Xièxiè!*]

*The greeting continues in English:*

Good morning [afternoon, evening], ladies and gentlemen: Our plane is descending now. Please be seated and fasten your seatbelt. Seat backs and tables should be returned to the upright position. All personal computers and electronic devices should be turned off. And please make sure that your carry-on items are securely stowed. We will be dimming the cabin lights for landing. Thank you!

*Both announcements can be shortened to accommodate a briefer transition between scenes.*

*The sound of a plane beginning to descend.*

## *2. SHANGHAI*

CELESTE *moves past the sights and sounds of Shanghai airport. A cacophony of sound and image.*

CELESTE: [*to the audience*] Shanghai airport.

*Almost without noticing, she begins to sing to herself … The* AIR HOSTESS *catches up to her.*

AIR HOSTESS: I didn't know you were a singer, Celeste!

CELESTE: Oh no, I'm not … it's just … if I'm a bit nervous sometimes … it helps me calm …

AIR HOSTESS: Are you sure your grandmother is coming?

CELESTE: Papa said Por Por would meet me. But … [*more nervous*] I can't see her anywhere.

*A box spins to reveal* POR POR*, carrying a large yellow sunflower.*

POR POR: Little Cloud! Celeste!

CELESTE: [*relieved*] Por Por! [*To the* AIR HOSTESS] That's her!

POR POR: [*to the* AIR HOSTESS] Thank you for looking after Little Cloud!

*She realises the* AIR HOSTESS *doesn't seem to understand.*

[*More slowly*] Thank You For Looking After Little Cloud!

CELESTE: [*to* POR POR] She can't speak Chinese, Por Por. Only English. [*To the* AIR HOSTESS] She said … thank you for looking after me.

AIR HOSTESS: You speak Chinese?

CELESTE: [*nodding*] I'm half Chinese, like Mama, and half French, like Papa. And all Australian!

POR POR *hands the sunflower to the* AIR HOSTESS. *They smile at each other.*

AIR HOSTESS: [*as she leaves*] Have a great stay in China, Celeste. [*To* POR POR] Thank You For My Flower!

CELESTE *waves goodbye as* POR POR *gently touches her cheek.*

POR POR: You look just like your mama.

*Beat.*

Tell me, how is your papa and little Robbie.

CELESTE: [*to the audience*] I don't want to tell her that since Mama died, Robbie can't sleep and Papa doesn't paint anymore. So instead I say, [*to* POR POR, *with a small smile*] they're fine.

POR POR *looks at her carefully for a moment and takes her hand.*

I can't wait to see your home.

*As* POR POR *grabs* CELESTE*'s bag, the scene transition begins.* CELESTE *and* POR POR *walk through the space as the set shifts around them.*

## *3. BIG MOUTH*

*The gates of Por Por's home.* CELESTE *looks about her.*

CELESTE: [*to the audience*] We're here.

*Beat.*

Por Por's house. I smell garlic, sizzling. Hear water, bubbling … And see …

POR POR: [*calling*] Ting Ting!

*A box spins around to reveal an older girl,* TING TING, *practising martial arts moves with precision. Seeing them,* TING TING *stops and comes to* POR POR. *She stands straight and tall. Not a hint of a smile.* CELESTE *and* TING TING *face each other.*

[*Smiling and jovial*] Ting Ting. Meet Celeste. Celeste … meet Ting Ting.

CELESTE: Hello.

TING TING: [*unsmiling*] Hello.

POR POR: [*seeming not to notice the tension*] I hope you two can become good friends. Ting Ting, show Celeste the fish pond while I water the *penjing*!

*As* POR POR *leaves,* TING TING *gracefully gestures* CELESTE *into the courtyard.*

CELESTE: [*to the audience*] A paved courtyard! There's a flying bat pattern at each corner … Tiny twisted trees growing from ancient stone pots …

*She is delighted, so much to see, wherever she looks …*

And a goldfish pond with strange symbols carved on the side! They look like ancient characters!

*Goldfish swirl about the stage.*

Look at the goldfish! Robbie would love this! All different sizes and colours!

TING TING: [*mocking*] Look at the goldfish …

CELESTE *turns. Is Ting Ting teasing her?*

CELESTE: Pardon?

TING TING: Nothing. See that big red fish. Ask if he's hungry.

CELESTE: What? No. I'd feel silly. Talking to a fish.

TING TING: Go on. He can understand human talk. Ask him.

CELESTE *looks at her suspiciously, but* TING TING *seems genuine. She leans towards the fish.*

CELESTE: Um … [*To the fish*] Are you hungry? [*To* TING TING] I don't think he's listening …

TING TING: [*persuasive*] Get closer. Lean right over the water and ask. He'll answer you. Go on.

*After a moment's hesitation,* CELESTE *does.*

Closer …

CELESTE *leans closer.*

Closer … that's it, ask now.

CELESTE: [*to the fish*] Can you hear me, Red Fish? Are. You. Hungry?

TING TING *darts away as a great spurt of water hits* CELESTE *in the face.*

CELESTE *chokes and splutters,* TING TING *laughs in delight.*

He splashed me! Yuck. That water stinks!

POR POR: [*entering*] Ting Ting! Celeste! [*Seeing them*] Making friends? Good.

*She glances at* CELESTE*'s wet face but says nothing.*

*A pause. Is Celeste going to dob on Ting Ting?*

I can leave you with Ting Ting while I get our tickets for home.

CELESTE: Tickets? I thought we *were* home.

POR POR: [*with a smile*] The Isle of Clouds. Your mama's true home.

POR POR *exits.* CELESTE *waves, looks for* TING TING. *She's gone too.* CELESTE *is alone with the fish. A moment. She feels small. A splash from the big fish.*

CELESTE: [*calling*] Ting Ting! Wait for me!

*And* CELESTE *goes into the house, calling after* TING TING *as she does.*

## *4. THE WRETCHED THING*

*In the house, calm quiet, dark.*

CELESTE *looks about.*

CELESTE: Hello? Ting Ting?

*No answer. In the half light we may see* TING TING *following* CELESTE *about, watching her, keeping out of view.*

[*To the audience*] Por Por's house is old and made of wood. It smells of … calm … and smoky tea. She has framed pictures from long ago.

*She looks at one with a smile.*

A little girl with black plaits and a cheeky grin …

*She sees another, bittersweet.*

And this one, Por Por and Mama.

*A humming/buzzing sound draws her attention.*

There's something here. Behind this door. It sounds like … a thousand bees …

*Lights change. A glow. She looks about in wonder.*

Wow. Weird stuff! Jars of herbs and powders, sticks and bones, bells and mirrors … and a sword, made of coins!

*She carefully picks up the coin sword. Behind her* TING TING *is still watching, creeping behind her.*

And everywhere, painted characters and strange symbols—like the writing around the fish pond outside. Strange. I feel like I've seen it before, but how could I?

*She puts the sword back down.*

Did I dream it? Maybe all the bits of dream are still floating in my head?

TING TING *and* CELESTE *touch hands. The two girls shout.*

Ow!

TING TING: Ah!

*Lights go back to normal.*

CELESTE: Why are you following me?!

TING TING: [*furious*] Why are you poking your nose into other people's business?! This room is private! For me and Por!

CELESTE: I'm just looking.

TING TING: You should never have come here. You think you're so special! Just because you're her *granddaughter*. Well, it doesn't mean anything, it doesn't mean you can do it!

CELESTE: Do what?!

*They are interrupted by the sound of a bicycle bell as* MRS WANG *enters.*

MRS WANG: Mrs Bao … I need Madame Bao! Quickly!

CELESTE: I'm sorry. Por Por's not here.

TING TING: [*calmly taking control*] I am in charge, Mrs Wang. How can I help?

MRS WANG: [*wailing*] Oh, Ting Ting! It's back! That wretched thing is back!

CELESTE: [*to* TING TING] What … wretched thing? What's she talking about?

TING TING: [*ignoring* CELESTE] Don't worry, Mrs Wang. I can take care of it. Ghost bag!

*Her ghost bag flies through the air and she slings it over her shoulder.*

MRS WANG: Oh, thank you, Ting Ting, thank you.

TING TING: Let's go!

*They start to leave.*

CELESTE: [*slightly panicked*] Ting Ting! Where are you going?

TING TING: [*calling as they leave*] Tell Por, I'm riding to Mrs Wang's. She needs me.

CELESTE: But [*weakly*] you don't have a bike helmet!

*They have gone.*

*A quiet moment.* CELESTE, *worried and afraid.*

Should I call the police? Or at least, an adult? Maybe Ting Ting's right, maybe I shouldn't have come. And … what was in that secret room?

POR POR *enters, wheeling her bicycle.*

POR POR: I'm home! Celeste! Ting Ting! I have the tickets! We're all set to leave for the Isle of Clouds, tomorrow!

*She sees* CELESTE*'s face.*

Where is Ting Ting?

CELESTE: She went with Mrs Wang.

POR POR: Mrs Wang?

CELESTE: Mrs Wang wanted *you*. She said it was urgent. She said …

*She stops to think.*

POR POR: Yes?

CELESTE: 'The wretched thing is back.'

*Beat.*

POR POR: I need my ghost bag …

*Her ghost bag flies through the air and she catches it.* POR POR *heads to her bicycle.*

Get on the back, Celeste.

CELESTE *climbs on the back. They begin to ride away. The following exchange takes place on the bicycle. This sequence is a fixed bike in profile. Filmed tracking shot of streets of Shanghai's French Colonial district.*

Mrs Wang lives in the French Quarter.

CELESTE: What's the French Quarter?

POR POR: This whole area of Shanghai used to belong to the French for almost a hundred years. They built houses just like the houses back home.

CELESTE: But why did the French own it when it's in China?

POR POR: At that time, China was very weak, so countries like England, France and America decided they would come in and grab a share. No country, and no person, can be strong forever, Little Cloud. They are strong for a time and weak for a time.

*Pause.*

CELESTE: Por Por … I don't think Ting Ting likes me very much.

POR POR: She's shy.

CELESTE: [*surprised*] Shy? I don't think so. Has she always lived with you?

POR POR: Since she was a very little girl. Her mother and father were killed in a bus accident many years ago. I took her in and she has been here ever since.

CELESTE: Poor Ting Ting!

POR POR: Yes, poor Ting Ting. Here we are!

*The sequence comes to an end as they make their way to the house of Mrs Wang.*

## *5. LES LETTRES SECRETES*

*Mrs Wang's house.*

CELESTE *and* POR POR *arrive.*

CELESTE: [*to the audience, nervous*] We stop in the rich part of town. Where the houses are huge! Mrs Wang's house is like a one-eyed monster staring down at us. Only one light flickers in an upstairs window. The house feels strange, like it's holding its breath. But for what?

*Inside the house, a staircase leads up to a door.*

*During the following scene the ghost fighting occurs offstage. Onstage there are a series of 'earth tremors' caused by the ghost, that unbalance the characters, indicated with the word 'shake'.*

MRS WANG: [*anxious*] Madame Bao, thank goodness, you are here at last.

*Shake.*

It's up there.

CELESTE: What was that?

*Distant roaring, in distorted French, comes from the top of the stairs.*

GHOST VOICE: *Parle-moi en français! Parle-moi en français!*

TING TING: [*offstage*] I can't understand you! Speak Chinese!

*Shake.*

POR POR: [*calm*] At least we know where Ting Ting is … Stay here, Little Cloud.

*And to* CELESTE*'s horror,* POR POR *carefully begins to walk up the staircase.*

CELESTE: Por Por, wait!

*She runs after her.*

We can get help! We can ring the police!

GHOST VOICE: *Stupide petite fille!*

CELESTE: [*calling*] Mrs Wang! Call the police! Please, my grandmother could get hurt!

*Shake.*

POR POR: Ting Ting! Come out of the room!

*Shake.*

Come out, Ting Ting, quickly.

TING TING: [*calling*] I can do this, give me a chance, Por!

POR POR: Leave. Now!

TING TING *emerges, resentfully joining* CELESTE *on the stairs under* POR POR.

[*Soothingly, as one might speak to an enraged dog*] It's alright. It's alright. I am here to help you.

*Shake.*

GHOST VOICE: *Trouve les papiers! Vite! Vite! Vite!*

POR POR: Shhh! Shhh! I am sorry. I don't know what you want. I can't understand what you are saying.

*Shake.*

TING TING: [*to* CELESTE] He can't speak Chinese. He only speaks French.

CELESTE: [*to* TING TING] French?! But … I'm half French! I can understand!

GHOST VOICE: *Où sont les papiers?!*

CELESTE *suddenly leaps up the staircase towards* POR POR.

CELESTE: I speak French, Por Por! I speak French! Tell him to talk to me! *Je parle français!*

POR POR: Careful, Celeste. What does he say …?

GHOST VOICE: *Les papiers sont derrière une brique dans le cheminée! Détruis les papiers avant qu'on les vole.*

CELESTE: [*translating*] He says … there are some papers behind a loose brick in the old fireplace. They must be destroyed, before they are stolen.

POR POR: Tell him: I will find the papers and destroy them. Then he can rest.

POR POR *draws her coin sword from her bag and enters the room.* CELESTE *remains outside the door.*

CELESTE: *Ma grand-mère va détruire les papiers pour toi. Tu peaux te reposer.*

TING TING: [*alarmed*] Por! [*To* CELESTE] What is she doing?

CELESTE: [*looking into the room*] She's going into the old brick fireplace. It's huge! She doesn't even have to bend her head!

GHOST VOICE: *La brique est plus haute. … oui celle-la!*

CELESTE: He says the brick is higher up, Por Por. Yes! That one.

*Beat.*

Oh!

TING TING: What?!

CELESTE: She's putting her arm into the hole in the fireplace. Ergh! There could be spiders!

TING TING: Don't be a coward!

CELESTE: If you ever come to Australia, I've got two words for you: Funnel. Web.

*Shake.*

She found them! [*Turning to* TING TING, *excited*] She found the papers!

TING TING: [*with contempt*] What did you expect?

CELESTE: [*calling*] *Reposez-vous, monsieur!*

*A flash of light, as the French ghost is captured by* POR POR *inside the house.*

What was that?!

POR POR *passes a bundle of papers out to* CELESTE.

[*Looking at them*] *Duck l'orange, île flotante, ratatouille, coq-au-vin, les escargot, bœuf bourguignon, pot-au-feu.* The papers are …

MRS WANG: Recipes?

POR POR: He was a famous chef. These recipes were hidden from his rival. Another chef, like him. Now, his secret recipes are forever safe … and he is at peace.

MRS WANG: Thank you, Madame Bao!

MRS WANG *offers* POR POR *a red envelope and exits.* POR POR *gives the wrapped mirror to* TING TING.

POR POR: Ting Ting, here you are. Don't drop the ming-shen mirror!

CELESTE: What if he gets angry again?

POR POR: He won't, Little Cloud.

TING TING: [*to* POR POR] You know I could have done it. I didn't need to understand what he was saying to stop him. How can I learn properly if you don't give me a chance to prove myself?

POR POR: You need to learn discipline and self-control first.

TING TING: Rubbish! You just think I'm not good enough because … she's here.

POR POR *exits to get her bike.*

CELESTE: Are you talking about me?

TING TING: Yes! You! You ruin everything. Why are you even here? We don't need you!

CELESTE: That's not fair.

TING TING: You don't even know what you are!

CELESTE: What do you mean? I'm half French, half Chinese …

TING TING: [*scornful*] Half of this, half of that. That just means you're not really anything. Here!

TING TING *angrily shoves the mirror at her and storms off.* POR POR *re-enters with the bike*

CELESTE: [*to* POR POR] I told you. She hates me.

POR POR: No. She's … tired. [*Yawning*] Me too.

CELESTE: Por Por, what was wrong with that French man? Where has he gone? And why did you need a coin sword?

POR POR: Too many questions for your old Por Por. We have a big bus journey tomorrow, to the Isle of Clouds. Come, we have to go home, eat, sleep and … see the fish pond.

CELESTE: Fish pond?

POR POR: That's what I said. One more thing … Don't drop that mirror!

*Music and lighting change.* POR POR *and* CELESTE *stay on stage as the bike is taken and the set changes around them to create a bus stop.*

## *6. THE BUS RIDE*

*Morning.*

POR POR *and* CELESTE *are waiting.* CELESTE *has her backpack.* POR POR *has her bag and an umbrella.* CELESTE *is impatient.* POR POR *is quiet, eyes closed.*

*A crack of distant thunder.* CELESTE *looks up. Oh no.*

*In one smooth action* POR POR *puts up her umbrella.*

CELESTE: You think of everything.

POR POR: [*opening her eyes*] No. But I give myself time to focus and wait for the mud in the water to settle.

CELESTE: Will Ting Ting be alright? Will she come to the Isle of Clouds?

POR POR: I left her ticket on the table. She knows how to look after herself. She has done so since she was very little.

*The rumbling, backfiring sound of a bus approaching.* CELESTE *turns and sees it.*

CELESTE: [*to the audience, alarmed*] The bus! It's old. I mean *really* old. It looks like a fat metal sausage … with a rusty roof and cracked windows.

DRIVER: 上车! [*Shàng chē!*]

*The* ENSEMBLE *assemble as passengers on the bus and* POR POR *finds her seat.* CELESTE *clambers awkwardly aboard to join her grandmother.*

CELESTE: [*clambering over a passenger*] Sorry! [*Leaning in to* POR POR] The roof is full of holes!

POR POR: Then we don't need to open a window!

*Another crack of thunder. It begins to rain.*

CELESTE: [*to the audience*] Something cold drips on my head! When I look up I see water pouring through a gaping hole in the rusty roof! It's raining inside the bus. This would never happen in Australia!

*A beat then she grins.*

But I kind of like it! We're jigging along the …

*The* ENSEMBLE *bump.*

… bumpy road. It's dark outside …

*The* ENSEMBLE *lean back.*

… and I can feel the old bus strain to get up the mountains.

*The* ENSEMBLE *lean forward; umbrellas down.*

CELESTE *wipes a circle in the window.*

*Bus change direction 1.*

The floor of the bus is sloshing with muddy cold water …

*Bus change direction 2.*

… every time we go round a bend the water runs up and down, up and down … And then—!

CELESTE *screams and pulls up her legs.*

POR POR: What's wrong, Celeste?

CELESTE: Something jumped on my leg! Something heavy and wet and cold and … alive!

ENSEMBLE: [*making the sound of frogs*] Ribbit! Ribbit!

POR POR: Just a frog.

CELESTE: [*aghast*] A frog?

ENSEMBLE: Ribbit! Ribbit!

POR POR: [*correcting*] No. My mistake.

*Beat.*

A *family* of frogs, hitching a ride.

*She smiles.*

ENSEMBLE: Ribbit! Ribbit! Ribbit!

CELESTE: [*to the audience*] Por Por is right! [*She shudders.*] Huge frogs as big as a man's fist are jumping on everyone's legs! [*Looking around*], No-one else seems to care. I can't keep my legs up forever, so …

*Slowly, carefully, she puts her legs down. She takes a deep breath.*

I try hard to pretend that the frogs are just … large soft stones rolling about the floor.

*The tension in her face starts to go.*

*Beside her,* POR POR *quietly notes that* CELESTE *has overcome her fear. She is pleased. The bus slows …*

POR POR: Look, Celeste. The Isle of Clouds.

*The bus stops.*

CELESTE: [*to the audience, as they step off the bus*] Not really an island. A water town surrounded with mist, makes it look like it's floating on a sea of clouds.

POR POR: Come, Celeste. This way. Follow me, across the bridge.

POR POR *starts to walk over the bridge.*

CELESTE *takes a moment to look about. Mist swirling. She hugs her backpack.*

*She carefully takes out the box of Mama's ashes.*

CELESTE: [*to the audience*] So much has happened since I arrived, so much weird stuff. Maybe here in the Isle of Clouds, I'll finally dream about Mama.

*She starts to unwrap the box, stopping when she hears:*

POR POR: [*calling, distant*] Celeste!

CELESTE *hurriedly replaces the box in the backpack as she calls back to her.*

CELESTE: Coming, Por Por!

CELESTE *follows* POR POR *over the bridge.*

## *7. THE ISLE OF CLOUDS*

*Morning.*

*The Isle of Clouds is a traditional and very beautiful water town. A canal runs between wooden two-story dwellings.*

*As lights come up we distantly hear the voice of* LING FENG, *a vegetable seller.*

LING FENG: [*calling loudly*] Cabbages! Lotus root! Mushroom and water spinach!

*A window overlooking the canal opens.* CELESTE *leans out, amazed at the scene below.*

CELESTE: [*to the audience*] The Isle of Clouds is an Isle of Boats! The canal is like the main road. With boats … instead of cars. [*Pointing*] There … a boat piled with metal woks. And … another with thin, black birds with long, pointed beaks sitting on the deck.

LING FENG *stands on her boat holding the tiller, floating gently along the canal. She sees* CELESTE *hanging out the window.*

LING FENG *sings a folk song, such as the one below.*

LING FENG: [*singing*] 月儿弯弯照九州
渔船儿到处好停留
青山绿水风光好呀
鱼哥哥吹笛妹梳头
[*Crescent moon illuminates the town
Fishing boats park along the canals
How beautiful is the scenic mountain and water
Boatman plays dazi lady combs her hair*]

CELESTE: [*seeing* LING FENG] And that one—a woman singing as she sells vegetables!

LING FENG: Cabbages! Lotus root!

CELESTE *joins in.*

Mushroom and water spinach!

*Laughter. A window near* CELESTE *pops open.* POR POR *pokes her head out too.*

POR POR: Is that my friend Ling Feng? The singing cabbage seller?

LING FENG: [*looking up, delighted*] Bao Min! You're back!

POR POR: Yes. And you have met Celeste. She's from Australia.

LING FENG: I never realised Australians look so much like Chinese!

POR POR: [*laughing*] She's my granddaughter! Celeste, hand me the basket.

CELESTE *passes the basket.* POR POR *ties it to a rope and hands it to* CELESTE *to lower down.*

LING FENG *chooses vegetables and places them carefully into the basket.*

LING FENG: [*calling up to* POR POR] Have you heard about Bao Mansion yet? The new owners want to renovate. It will be Shanghai in the mountains! [*Placing the vegetables*] Cabbage and lotus root!

CELESTE: What is Bao Mansion?

LING FENG *gestures and* CELESTE *turns to see.*

LING FENG: Bao Mansion was beautiful once. But, it has changed—ever since it was cruelly taken from your Por Por's family. [*Adding to the basket*] Mushrooms and water spinach!

*The basket is raised to the window as* LING FENG *boats on.*

Goodbye, Bao Min! Let us play mah-jong soon! Goodbye, Celeste! [*Calling as she goes*] Cabbages! Lotus root! Mushroom and water spinach!

CELESTE: Por Por, what happened to Bao Mansion?

POR POR: First, eat, Little Cloud. I have made some rice porridge with fish.

*They sit at the window and eat.*

Bao Mansion was once the grandest house in the Isle Of Clouds.

*Music.*

*An animated version of* POR POR*'s story appears around them.*

My father, your great-grandfather, was Judge Bao. He was greatly respected by the people of this town. He was accused of stealing a large amount of money by a jealous man named Shen Da Pai. At first no-one believed him. But … like a worm creeping into one of Ling Feng's cabbages, he ate away at the truth until finally it became brown and rotten.

CELESTE: And what happened to your father?

*A slight pause.*

POR POR: He was arrested and taken to prison. It was the last day I ever saw him. He died there. His wealth and all belongings were taken away from our family.

CELESTE: [*horrified*] Your father! And your family!

POR POR: We were forced to leave Bao Mansion. I went to Shanghai to work as a maid. I was twelve years old. I sent money to my mother and little brothers for a long time, but one day the money came back. They had gone. Disappeared.

CELESTE: Where?

POR POR: [*sadly*] I don't know. I tried to find them. I searched. But, China is a big country.

MR GUO*, nervous, bespectacled, anxiously approaches on his bicycle. Strapped to his chest is a baby.*

MR GUO: Madame Bao. Thank goodness you are back in the Isle of Clouds!

POR POR: Mr Guo. Are you well?

MR GUO: Yes. That is … no! Strange things have been happening in my house. [*Looking around, unwilling to reveal more*] Please, Madame Bao, would you … could you …?

POR POR: [*understanding*] Mr Guo, would you like me to come and … examine the house?

MR GUO: Yes please, Madame Bao! If it's no trouble …

POR POR: No trouble. Go home, Mr Guo. We will be there soon.

MR GUO: Thank you!

MR GUO *climbs back on his bicycle and leaves.*

CELESTE: Why do these people ask for *you*, Por Por?

POR POR: Mr Guo came to me for help because … I am a ghost hunter.

CELESTE: [*bursting into laughter*] Ghost … hunter?

POR POR: Our family has done this for generations. Some are good at maths or literature. Our family is good at hunting ghosts.

CELESTE: But … there is no such thing as … ghosts. Everyone knows that.

POR POR: [*choosing her words carefully*] The gift is passed down through the females in the family … I believe … you may be a ghost hunter too, Celeste.

CELESTE: Me? I can't be! I'm afraid of the dark! I hate watching scary movies! And Mama, I tried to talk to Mama, she's never answered me.

POR POR: Your mother is at peace. She is not a ghost. She has no need to linger.

CELESTE: I don't know if I want to be a ghost hunter.

POR POR: [*with a sigh*] Neither did your mother.

*A moment as* CELESTE *looks over the canal.*

CELESTE: [*thinking*] Mama could have been a ghost hunter …?

POR POR: And so could you, Celeste …

CELESTE: [*grinning*] Then, does this mean … I get to use the coin sword?

POR POR: [*serious*] I told you, this is a gift. Not everyone who wants it, has it. And not everyone who has it, wants it.

*Beat.*

Come. We must get ready to go to Mr Guo's.

POR POR *heads back inside.* CELESTE *stands a moment, looking at the canal.*

CELESTE: Mama. Is this why I'm here in China? In the Isle of Clouds? Is this why you said I had to bring your ashes home?

*As* CELESTE *goes back inside the house, darkness falls.*

## *8. THE HOUSE OF MR GUO*

*Music changes to become more sinister.*

*A bed is placed on stage. This is the house of Mr Guo.*

POR POR *and* CELESTE *enter cautiously.* POR POR *has her sword and her ghost bag slung over one shoulder.*

CELESTE: [*to the audience*] The house of Mr Guo is … dark.

*On these last words, a huge black cloth drops—a kabuki drop.*

POR POR: Hold this, Celeste …

*She hands the sword to* CELESTE *and begins to rummage in her bag.*

*Holding the sword,* CELESTE *can feel the magic within.*

*She does a few experimental sweeps through the air.*

CELESTE: [*to the audience*] I can feel the sword tingling, through my arm. It's as if I know how to use this, I know how to fight with it!

POR POR *does not seem to hear but smiles to herself as she takes something out of her bag and hands it to* CELESTE.

POR POR: [*instructing her*] The ming-shen mirror is used to trap ghosts.

CELESTE *looks at it, wonderingly.* POR POR *abruptly covers the mirror.*

*Ayah!* Never look inside the mirror unless a ghost has been captured. If the mirror is empty, you may be trapped within forever.

*She finds a little box.*

Aha. My ghost revealing powder … And for you, Celeste … your weapons.

CELESTE*'s excitement is dampened somewhat as* POR POR *holds up … two bells.*

CELESTE: [*fighting her disappointment*] Bells? No sword?

POR POR: [*smiling*] No sword. Remember: a sword is not always the right weapon for the battle at hand.

CELESTE *hands back the mirror which* POR POR *carefully tucks back into the bag and, reluctantly, the coin sword.*

Hold the bells out, Celeste. One in each hand. Be ready …

*They take a few cautious steps forward,* CELESTE *holding up the bells in both arms.*

CELESTE: I feel like a chimpanzee.

POR POR: You sound like an elephant. Tread quietly! Shhh … there's definitely something here …

*The wistful sound of a flute.* CELESTE *looks about.*

CELESTE: Por Por? I hear someone playing a flute. It's beautiful …

POR POR: Perhaps. But can you hear the sound *behind* the flute?

*She produces the box of powder and, taking a handful, scatters it into the air.*

Ghost … reveal!

*Lights change to a corridor of light.*

*The bed lurches and the mattress ripples.* CELESTE, *terrified, and* POR POR, *stern, watch as the bed starts to vibrate up and down.*

Celeste! Ring the bells!

*As* CELESTE *rings her bells, the bed goes still and the shape of a figure appears under the sheets. We hear heavy breathing.* CELESTE *approaches cautiously. The bed lunges towards* CELESTE *who screams, the figure disappears and all is still.*

CELESTE: It's stopped.

CELESTE *approaches the bed and taps it with the bells. Nothing. She gives a sigh of relief. Carelessly, she pulls at the sheet. To her sudden horror, her arm is caught by the bed and trapped. She screams.*

POR POR: Move, Celeste! Away from the bed!

*But* CELESTE*'s arm is trapped and* POR POR *has to push her out of the way. The bed whips its sheet at* POR POR, *knocking her sword out of her hand. The bed looms over* POR POR *who holds up her hands as if holding it back.*

CELESTE: Por Por! Por Por!

POR POR *is sucked underneath the bed and disappears!*

*And then, somehow …* CELESTE *begins to sing her ghost song, at first tentative and then stronger. Her ghost song is wordless, a powerful surge of sound. As* CELESTE *sings, the bed stops bucking, arches up into a contorted position, and the sheet goes still. The song ends.*

POR POR *emerges from the bed, picking up her coin sword.*

*Thinking she has won,* CELESTE *turns back to* POR POR *in triumph.*

Por Por! Did you see? Did you hear?

*At that moment, the drumming restarts, the bed rears up again, charging one last time. The sheet shoots out and wraps around* CELESTE. POR POR *takes up a position with sword and mirror.*

POR POR: [*chanting and using the coin sword*] Ghost be gone! Ghost be gone!

*The bed falls back, the drumming abruptly stops. The sheet falls from* CELESTE.

POR POR *takes out the ming-shen mirror and holds it high.*

Ghost be gone …!

*A bright light 'zaps' the mirror in* POR POR*'s hands.*

*Then, silence. Lights change.*

CELESTE *can't believe what she has just experienced.*

CELESTE: It worked, Por Por. It's gone!

POR POR *gives the mirror to* CELESTE.

POR POR: *Now* you can look.

CELESTE: [*holding the mirror carefully*] There's something in here … faint, shimmery, blob.

MR GUO *emerges. He bows as he hands* POR POR *a red envelope.*

MR GUO: Thank you, Madame Bao. My family and I are grateful.

POR POR: Who was the ghost, Mr Guo?

MR GUO: My grandmother's older brother. He lived here for the last thirty years. We called him Uncle Cranky. He used to complain the bed was too hard.

CELESTE: He died here? In this house?

MR GUO: In his sleep. Thank you, Madame Bao. And thank you to your apprentice!

MR GUO *leaves, taking the bed and sheet with him.*

POR POR *takes the mirror from* CELESTE, *putting it back in the bag.*

POR POR: We will take this ghost home with us.

CELESTE: Home?

POR POR: We have a pond for naughty ghosts. Just like the one in Shanghai.

CELESTE: But that pond didn't have ghosts, it had [*realising*] fish! Por Por! Are all the fish in your pond ghosts?

POR POR: [*nodding*] That is where they learn to be … humble.

CELESTE: [*hesitant*] Por Por … I was so scared.

POR POR: [*looking at her, seriously*] Yes, you were.

CELESTE: [*forlorn*] I thought that ghost bed was going to hurt you. [*Thinking*] But that's when … I began to sing. It was like … everything I've felt since I came here to China—about family and home and … losing Mama—it suddenly came pouring out of me like a waterfall, but I couldn't control it …

POR POR: [*nodding*] You need to control that power. [*Smiling*] Still, I have never heard of a ghost hunter using a ghost song before. Tomorrow, we rest. Shopping. Eating. Sightseeing.

*She rubs at her shoulder.*

Acupuncture.

CELESTE: [*disappointed*] No ghosts?

POR POR: No ghosts!

CELESTE: Maybe … we could … scatter Mama's ashes tomorrow, Por Por.

POR POR: [*gently*] Not yet, Little Cloud. It's not yet the right time.

CELESTE: Then, could we see your childhood home? Bao Mansion.

POR POR: Of course.

POR POR *exits.* CELESTE *pauses a moment, feeling the elation of the moment.*

CELESTE: [*to the audience*] Por Por said she'd never heard of a ghost hunter using a ghost song before. Celeste LaClaire. Apprentice ghost hunter!

*Clumsily she attempts the ghost-fighting moves.*

That's me! Maybe I can get it on a t-shirt …

*She follows* POR POR. *A beat then a figure emerges.* TING TING. *Angry. And hurt.*

TING TING: You think you're so special.

*She mimics Celeste's clumsy ghost-fighting moves.*

Celeste LaClaire. Apprentice ghost hunter! And what's a ghost song anyway?

*She busts out an awesome sequence of ghost-fighting moves.*

*I'm* meant to be Por's apprentice. Not you.

*A second kabuki drop reveals …*

*9. BAO MANSION*

*A spectacular tracking shot through a water town frames* CELESTE *and* POR POR *on the back of a water taxi, alongside a* BOATMAN. *They have bags from their morning's shopping.*

CELESTE: [*to the audience*] Por Por and I go to the marketplace on a water taxi. We zip through the green canal water. Por Por goes to the acupuncture clinic and I keep shopping.

BOATMAN: [*to the audience, dryly*] Lots of shopping.

CELESTE: [*to the audience*] I buy this …

*She rummages in the bag and holds it up.*

… a kazoo, for my little brother Robbie. He's always wanted one.

*She toots a few notes and puts it in her pocket.*

I miss him. [*Realising*] I miss everyone.

POR POR *sits beside* CELESTE *and takes her hand, holding it in her lap.*

POR POR: [*to* CELESTE] Celeste! Do you see over there, Mount Mystery? Its peak is only visible a few times each year. We will go there when it's time to scatter your mother's ashes.

*A moment between them.*

CELESTE: [*to the audience*] Por Por understands me. She's the wisest and kindest person I know.

BOATMAN: 下一站 … 宝家大宅 . [*Bǎo jiā dàzhái.*]

POR POR: I'll get the bags.

*She turns upstage to get the bags.*

CELESTE: That looks like … Ting Ting!

*She waves frantically.*

Ting Ting! Ting Ting! It's me, Celeste! Ting Ting! She's gone.

BOATMAN: 宝家大宅! 宝家大宅! [*Bǎo jiā dàzhái! Bǎo jiā dàzhái!*]

POR POR *emerges and ushers* CELESTE *off the boat.*

CELESTE: Por Por, I saw Ting Ting. Back on the bridge. I think she saw me.

POR POR: Good. She must have found the ticket I left in Shanghai.

CELESTE: Shouldn't we go back and get her?

POR POR: She'll find us. Now …

*She stops, looks around.*

Celeste. This is Bao Mansion.

CELESTE *looks around, amazed at what she sees.*

CELESTE: Por Por. It's so beautiful!

POR POR: [*pointing*] You see that window up there? That was my bedroom.

CELESTE: [*to the audience*] There are fish carved around the window! I can almost see Por Por, that cheeky little girl with black plaits, laughing, looking out.

POR POR: [*pointing again*] Over there, the lake with life-giving powers, spring water so pure you can drink it. This was once such a beautiful garden …

MRS TAN: … and it will be again.

POR POR *and* CELESTE *turn in surprise.* MRS TAN *is young and groovy, with long boots.*

POR POR: I am sorry, I am Bao Min and this is my granddaughter Celeste visiting from Australia …

MRS TAN: Madame Bao! I have heard so much about you. You wanted to see the old mansion, of course! Welcome. I am Tan Yi, my husband and I are the new owners. I wanted to meet you and ask about the origins of this beautiful old home. The people who lived here before me, the Shen family, left years ago.

POR POR: I would be honoured.

MRS TAN: Thank you. I'll make us some tea.

POR POR: Thank you, Mrs Tan.

MRS TAN *goes into the house.* POR POR *turns to* CELESTE.

There is something you should know. Mrs Tan mentioned 'the Shen family'. This is the family of Shen Da Pai. Bao Mansion has been with the Shen family ever since our family was forced to leave …

CELESTE: What happened to the Shen family?

POR POR: They moved to Shanghai. And then, one day, when their daughter was at school, the two parents were killed in a bus accident.

CELESTE: That's terrible.

POR POR: Yes. That is why I took in their little girl to live with me.

CELESTE: [*realising*] Ting Ting? But then, that means …

POR POR: Yes. Her real name is Shen Ting Ting. She is the granddaughter of Shen Da Pai. Promise me something, Celeste. You must never tell Ting Ting that her grandfather was the cause of my father's imprisonment and death. A secret between you and me. Yes?

CELESTE: Yes, Por Por. I promise.

POR POR *smiles and takes her hand.*

POR POR: Come, we will see where your Por Por was once that little girl with the black plaits and the cheeky laugh. Follow me …

POR POR *exits.* CELESTE *stays onstage as the* ENSEMBLE *transform the space, using white sheets, into Bao Mansion.*

## *10. THE FIRST BATTLE*

*The interior of Bao Mansion is dark, formal-looking. One latticed window high above shows the day gradually becoming evening.*

CELESTE: [*to the audience*] Inside Bao Mansion there are high ceilings held up by thick, dark-red pillars. White sheets are thrown over furniture piled high in the corner.

CELESTE *is relieved to see* MRS TAN *and* POR POR *enter.*

MRS TAN: … so that was where we'll have the tearoom, and the room on the other side will be the lobby. We are hoping to call the new spa hotel by its original name of Bao Mansion if that is alright with you, Madame Bao?

POR POR: It would please me very much … Thank you, Mrs Tan. You have been very kind to show us around. Celeste, ready to go?

MRS TAN: I … wanted to speak to you about something before you go, Madame Bao.

*A slight pause. A creaking noise.* MRS TAN *looks around nervously.*

I am told … you, ah … have some experience with um …

*Pause.*

CELESTE: Ghosts?

MRS TAN *hesitates.*

POR POR: Go on.

*The creaking noise again.*

MRS TAN: Noises. Wind where there is no wind. Footsteps when there should be no-one else here. Things move, Madame Bao, shutters, furniture …

POR POR: It's alright. Pack your things, stay at the hotel. I will send for you when it is over.

MRS TAN: Thank you, Madame Bao, thank you.

MRS TAN *leaves.*

CELESTE: She was scared.

POR POR: [*nodding*] It may be nothing. Mrs Tan may simply have a nervous disposition. I just want to check.

*She stands in the centre of the room, eyes closed, hands outstretched.*

Stay close, Celeste. Stay alert.

POR POR *walks with her hands outstretched before her. A gentle wind ripples the fabric of the walls. As* CELESTE *moves closer, a flute begins to play. She looks up, wary.*

CELESTE: I hear music, flute music …

POR POR: Shhh. Stop talking.

POR POR *disappears from the stage.* CELESTE, *still frozen, misses seeing her go. She is alone.*

CELESTE: Por Por?

*Drumming begins, slow and sinister.*

CELESTE *sees something at the window and gasps.*

[*Calling*] Por Por! Where are you?! The ghost is here! I can see it!

POR POR: [*running back in*] You can see it? Where?

CELESTE: There! [*Pointing*] By the window. Like a shadow. An old man in a long robe. He's holding … a black feather in one hand and his fingernails are long and pointed.

*Projected through the window screen is the shadow of Shen Da Pai.*

POR POR: Shen Da Pai! [*Starting her protection mudra movements*] Protection mudra. Do it with me, Little Cloud! Quickly!

CELESTE *tries, but gets flustered.*

CELESTE: I can't, Por Por.

*She looks around.*

I can't see him! He's gone …

*Suddenly* TING TING *runs in, taking up her position on the other side of* POR POR.

POR POR: Ting Ting! Ten-star mudra! Do it with me now.

TING TING *and* POR POR *work the mudra movements in unison.*

CELESTE: The ghost! I see him! He's over there! He's pointing the feather at … Ting Ting!

TING TING *staggers and falls.* CELESTE *tries to help her up.*

*From left: Alice Keohavong as Celeste, Amanda Ma as Por Por and Yilin Kong as Ting Ting in Barking Gecko's production in 2018. (Photo: Daniel Grant)*

POR POR: Ting Ting! Don't stop the mudra!

CELESTE: Por Por, watch out! He's pointing again! At you!

*The drumming is louder.* POR POR *staggers and begins to chant.*

POR POR: Ghost be gone. Ghost be gone. Ghost be gone.

CELESTE: [*pointing forward*] Now he's there!

*As* POR POR *chants,* TING TING *struggles to resume the mudra. She shouts at* CELESTE.

TING TING: Por is getting weaker! Do something!

CELESTE: I can't!

TING TING: What about your famous ghost song?! Use that!

CELESTE: I can't control it!

POR POR *staggers again. Her chanting is getting weaker.* TING TING *glances at her, worried.*

TING TING: You have to do *something*. Now!

CELESTE *suddenly begins to sing, advancing on Shen Da Pai with her song.*

*Suddenly, there is a great wave of light, the drumming stops.*

The ghost! It's gone!

CELESTE: But where?

TING TING: It doesn't matter. It's gone. He was strong, I could feel his power. But we did it, Por!

POR POR: [*nodding, weakened*] You both did well. But that was only the first battle. He will be back. [*To* TING TING] It is good to have you with us again. We need to go home. So I can prepare.

CELESTE: So we can *all* prepare, Por Por. All of us.

POR POR: It will just be me who returns. You were right, Ting Ting. This ghost is strong. Neither of you are ready to face him.

TING TING: [*simultaneously*] What?! No, Por!

CELESTE: [*simultaneously*] Por Por!

TING TING: When I said he was strong I didn't mean I couldn't fight him! I've seen plenty of ghosts and fought them and turned them into goldfish.

POR POR: [*calm*] This ghost cannot be turned into a goldfish. It must be dissolved.

*A slight pause as they realise what she means by this.*

Decision is final.

*She leaves.*

TING TING: [*to* CELESTE] Did Por teach you that ghost song? [*Begrudgingly*] It was good. Enough.

CELESTE: Thanks. I think.

POR POR: [*calling*] Ting Ting! Celeste!

*And a disappointed* CELESTE *and outraged* TING TING *hurry after her.*

## *11. THE SECRET COMES OUT*

*Home by the canal.*

POR POR *appears in her room, praying.*

*The noisy rattle of small stones.* TING TING *and* CELESTE *are revealed, attempting to play the board game weiqi, but stealing anxious looks towards* POR POR.

TING TING: [*gesturing at the door*] Por always prays for her enemies. [*Glancing at the board*] You're winning! Have you played weiqi before? How did you do that?

CELESTE: [*with a shrug*] You need to be calm and see the bigger picture …

*She places more stones on the board.*

Por Por said she wanted to pray for the ghost in Bao Mansion.

TING TING: That's it!

*She throws her stones down.*

I've had enough weiqi.

CELESTE: Hey! I was winning.

TING TING *moves to the door, planning to eavesdrop.* CELESTE *collects the stones up.*

What are you doing?

TING TING: What does it look like I'm doing? I want to know who that ghost is.

*She puts her ear to the door and listens. She steps back, confused, but gradually growing in anger.*

CELESTE: What did you hear?

TING TING: She's praying for … my grandfather. Shen Da Pai. But, he can't have been the ghost. That ghost was evil.

*She glares at* CELESTE *who is silent, horrified.*

My grandfather doesn't need Por to pray for him! He was very well respected. Unlike her father … Judge Bao.

CELESTE: [*angry, she can't let this go*] That's not true! Because of *your* grandfather, Por Por and her entire family were thrown out of Bao Mansion. Shen Da Pai *killed* Por Por's father by having him put into gaol for something he didn't do.

TING TING: [*insistent*] Por's father was the bad one.

CELESTE: No! Shen Da Pai tried to destroy our family. That's the *truth*. Por Por knows it. I know it … and you know it too.

TING TING: I know … everything was fine until *you* came along.

*And she storms out.*

*A frozen moment.*

CELESTE *hears* POR POR *coming back out.*

*She sits back in front of the weiqi table.* POR POR *glances at her.*

POR POR: Playing weiqi? [*Looking about*] Where's Ting Ting?

CELESTE: [*shamefaced*] I don't know. We … had an argument.

POR POR: Mmm. She doesn't like to lose.

*Beat.*

Never mind. I have decided that tomorrow you need some ghost practice.

CELESTE: Ghost practice?! [*Worried*] With … a real ghost?

POR POR: It will be daylight. And I am going to give you some things you can use.

*She holds up a long, twisted stick.*

CELESTE: A stick.

POR POR: A lightning stick.

*She wipes it fondly with her sleeve.*

It was your mother's. It has never been used …

CELESTE: *A lightning stick*? What's that?

POR POR: You use it to catch a Fat Belly Ghost. When a person dies, their soul has forty-nine days to pass through to the underworld. If the soul loses its way … it can get stuck. That is a Fat Belly Ghost! [*Solemnly*] Now. Do you want me to tell you the very first secret of ghost hunting? Something all ghost hunters must remember.

CELESTE: Yes! Please, Por Por!

POR POR: Crucial! Vital! Extremely important.

CELESTE: Tell me!

POR POR: Before you go and fight your ghost … remember: go to the toilet first!

POR POR *laughs.*

## *12. FAT BELLY GHOST*

CELESTE *stands by a large tree with wide, spreading branches.*

CELESTE: [*to the audience*] Por Por said I could catch the Fat Belly Ghost here by this ancient tree. But I don't even know what a Fat Belly Ghost looks like!

FAT BELLY GHOST: [*in the tree*] Pooo! What's that horrible smell?

CELESTE *turns cautiously towards the voice.*

CELESTE: Hello …

FAT BELLY GHOST: A stupid, stinky girl.

CELESTE *sees the* GHOST *inside the tree, glaring out at her.*

CELESTE: [*trying to stay calm and controlled*] My name is—Celeste …

FAT BELLY GHOST: Smelly Celeste! Pooo … you smell like a rotten egg!

CELESTE *looks for* POR POR *but she has gone.*

CELESTE: [*to the audience*] How do I get him into my mirror? It's impossible …

FAT BELLY GHOST: Boo hooo! Cry baby! You don't live here, do you? Where are you from?

CELESTE: Australia. It's a long way from here. What about you? Where do you live?

FAT BELLY GHOST: I don't live anywhere! I'm a ghost!

CELESTE: I know. I'm a ghost hunter.

FAT BELLY GHOST: You're too stupid to be a ghost hunter … Stupid and stinky!

CELESTE *and the* FAT BELLY GHOST *stare angrily at each other. Suddenly,* CELESTE *laughs.*

What's so funny?

CELESTE: You! You remind me of my little brother. Robbie. He's not as cheeky as you but I bet he'd love to be! [*She quietens.*] I miss him. [*She realises.*] You must miss your family too. Tell me what happened.

*Music. An animation of the following plays as the* FAT BELLY GHOST *tells the story.*

FAT BELLY GHOST: I lived on a boat. On the canal. I spent more time on water than dry land, with the wind in my face and the splash of the green canal water. My mother tied a rope around my waist at first so that I wouldn't fall off. When I was seven they took the rope off. I had perfect balance! One day, my mother and father were at the market. I was playing on the boat, and I slipped and banged my head hard. I sank down, down to the bottom. It was dark and cold. When my parents came back, it was too late.

CELESTE *is moved, tries to reach out to the* FAT BELLY GHOST *who has become quiet.*

CELESTE: Hey … My brother Robbie is seven, and he's cheeky and funny and brave, like you.

*A slight pause as she has an idea.*

Do you want to see what I bought Robbie at the markets?

*She shows him the kazoo.*

A kazoo! Listen …

*She buzzes on it but the* FAT BELLY GHOST *makes a face and, howling, claps his hands to his ears.*

FAT BELLY GHOST: Horrible!

*She buzzes again.*

Mosquito!

CELESTE: Sorry!

CELESTE *hastily puts the kazoo away.*

FAT BELLY GHOST: Tell more about Robbie.

CELESTE: Well … even though he's brave, he's too scared to sleep by himself.

FAT BELLY GHOST: That's not brave! That's like … a baby!

CELESTE: [*thinking*] No … He's scared if he goes to sleep, he might never wake up. [*Hesitant*] That's what happened with Mama. She … had an operation and she never woke up. I miss her every day. I think of all the things we never said to each other—about China, about Por Por. All the things we'll never do together—shopping and playing music and speaking Chinese. And saying … I love you.

*She stops. She takes a breath, looks at the* FAT BELLY GHOST.

You miss them. Your family.

*A slight pause.*

Do you want to be with them?

*The* FAT BELLY GHOST *nods.*

I can help you find the place you're meant to go. Come on.

CELESTE *carefully draws out the lightning stick. The sound of gentle humming. In her other hand she holds the ming-shen mirror. Carefully she moves the stick slowly from tree to mirror.*

*A flash of blinding light as the* FAT BELLY GHOST *is trapped in the ming-shen mirror. Faintly we hear the* FAT BELLY GHOST.

FAT BELLY GHOST: Goodbye, smelly Celeste. Goodbye!

CELESTE *smiles as she waves goodbye.*

*Lights normalise. The* FAT BELLY GHOST *is gone.* POR POR *is there.*

POR POR: [*gently*] Well done, Little Cloud. Your mama would be proud.

CELESTE: [*handing the mirror to* POR POR] He won't go in the fish pond, will he?

POR POR: No. We guide him to the door that leads to the underworld. This [*showing* CELESTE *a small paper lantern*] is the Hu Lantern. Wherever it lands is the entrance to the underworld. It will take him where he needs to go.

POR POR *holds the mirror up above the lantern. From the ming-shen mirror comes the blue light of the Fat Belly Ghost. The blue light transfers to the lantern which now glows from the inside.*

*Holding out the lantern,* POR POR *releases it and it floats, glowing blue, up and across the stage until finally it disappears.*

CELESTE: He's gone home. [*A sad smile, she is missing home too*] Por Por, why do people have to die?

*In answer,* POR POR *puts her arms around* CELESTE.

LING FENG: [*offstage*] Bao Min! Bao Min!

POR POR *and* CELESTE *turn to see* TING TING *beaten and bloodied, helped by* LING FENG.

POR POR: What has happened?

TING TING: I went to Bao Mansion. I went to see the ghost of my grandfather, Shen Da Pai. Celeste told me what he did to your father.

CELESTE *looks away, ashamed.* POR POR *strokes* TING TING*'s head.*

I didn't want to believe her. But it was all true.

POR POR: You should not have gone, it was too dangerous.

TING TING: [*becoming tearful*] He was so angry. All the windows smashed and glass flew through the air.

LING FENG: Bao Min, we must take the girl to hospital.

TING TING: [*suddenly grasping at her neck*] My necklace! My talisman necklace. It's gone! What if he is using it against me?

CELESTE: It will be alright, Ting Ting.

TING TING: [*angrily*] Alright? How can it be?

POR POR: You must go to the hospital now.

LING FENG *helps* TING TING *away.* POR POR *turns to* CELESTE.

CELESTE: It's my fault, I told her the secret. I'm sorry.

POR POR: I must go to Bao Mansion. [*Sternly*] You will stay at home, Celeste. Wait for Ting Ting.

CELESTE: Por Por, I said I'm sorry!

POR POR, *ignoring her, leaves.*

[*To the audience*] I wish I wasn't so scared. I wish I could run away. I know what Mama would say: you can't run away, mistakes only catch up with you. [*Thinking*] But, maybe … there is *one* thing I can do.

*And, determined, she follows* POR POR *off stage right.*

## *13. RETURN TO BAO MANSION*

*Bao Mansion. Night.*

*A torch picks its way through the darkness. It's* CELESTE.

CELESTE: Por Por?

*Another torch can be seen moving through the darkness.*

[*Nervous*] Por Por … is that you?

TING TING: It's me.

CELESTE: Ting Ting! What are you doing in Bao Mansion? You're meant to be in hospital!

TING TING: I couldn't stay at the hospital. I came to help Por fight. What are *you* doing?

CELESTE: I followed her here. I hid by the lake of pure water when she came in. She didn't come out, so I came inside to find her.

TING TING: [*angry*] You let Por go in by herself? Call yourself a ghost hunter? You are such a coward!

CELESTE: [*stung at the injustice of the accusation*] Yeah, I'm *such* a coward. [*Holding up* TING TING*'s necklace*] I found *this*.

TING TING: My talisman necklace! You … found it!

CELESTE: Shen Da Pai had it hidden in his strongbox … with all sorts of horrible stuff.

TING TING: What kind of horrible stuff?

CELESTE: Claws. A black chicken feather. Clumps of hair and fur. The skull of a bird. Things that smell bad.

TING TING: Those are black talismans. They must have been given to him by a black magician. Por's in trouble. We have to find her. [*Begrudgingly*] Thanks … for getting my necklace back.

CELESTE: [*accepting*] Okay.

TING TING: But … it doesn't change anything. It's still all your fault.

CELESTE: [*understanding*] Let's go.

*They climb up the ladder, deeper into Bao Mansion.*

Por Por!

TING TING: Por!

CELESTE: [*worried*] Por Por's not anywhere.

TING TING: [*also worried, trying not to show it*] Something's happened. Let's look again, we *have* to find her.

*Looking around, she makes a discovery.*

A hidden room. And … [*backing away*] it stinks! You go in … I'll keep guard!

CELESTE *reluctantly climbs down into the secret room.*

[*Calling*] Hurry up. It's getting really cold out here …

*Her torch goes out.*

[*Calling*] Celeste, my torch just went out.

CELESTE*'s torch goes out too.*

CELESTE: [*calling back*] So did mine.

*A horrible laugh, like a knife scraping glass.*

[*Looking up*] Who's there?! Ting Ting! Where are you?

*Silence.* TING TING *has gone.*

Ting Ting? [*Calling desperately*] Por Por?!

*The voice, amplified, sinister, laughs again.*

SHEN DA PAI: [*voiceover, mocking*] 'Por Por'.
CELESTE: [*screaming, trying to see*] Keep away!

*The tall dark figure of* SHEN DA PAI *enters.*

SHEN DA PAI: Look around. There's no-one here to help you.
CELESTE: Where is Por Por?
SHEN DA PAI: What are you going to do, apprentice ghost hunter?

*Another horrible scornful laugh.*

*Furious,* CELESTE *begins to sing her ghost song.*

SHEN DA PAI *thrusts out an angry hand towards her and she falters … He laughs, sensing victory.*

Come on! You're angry, aren't you? Scared? Sad for your poor mama? She wasn't cut out to be a ghost hunter. And neither are you, Celeste.!
CELESTE: [*a sudden remembrance*] Por Por said I need to focus. Calm myself … let the mud settle.

*She breathes. Focusses. Begins the ghost song again. This time it is strong and powerful. She advances on him.*

*He is driven back and finally disappears out of sight, seemingly almost beaten.*

*Suddenly, a scream from* TING TING.

CELESTE *stops. Sudden silence. She whirls around.*

Ting Ting! Ting Ting! Where are you?

SHEN DA PAI *re-appears. He spreads one clawed hand towards* CELESTE.

CELESTE *gasps, chokes and clutches at her throat. She tries to sing again … but can't.*

*As* SHEN DA PAI *begins to rise, regaining strength,* CELESTE *stumbles away.*

*He reaches his hand towards her again and she chokes.*

*Suddenly she feels the kazoo in her pocket. She takes it out and begins to play.* SHEN DA PA*i is blown backwards, off the stage.*

TING TING *appears.*

TING TING: Celeste!

CELESTE: [*breathless*] Ting Ting! You're alive!

TING TING: Of course I'm alive! I was fighting Shen Da Pai. And I crushed him!

CELESTE: Um. No. *I* crushed him. With Robbie's kazoo.

TING TING: How can you crush him here when I'm crushing him upstairs?

CELESTE: It's not like there's two of them … [*A horrified realisation*] Are there?

*Two* SHEN DA PAI*s appear!*

There *are* two of them!

TING TING: Really powerful ghosts can split themselves in two.

SHEN DA PAI 1: Ting Ting. You are a Shen. Why are you fighting with Bao Min's granddaughter?

SHEN DA PAI 2: Join with me and find your true family.

CELESTE *looks nervously at* TING TING.

TING TING: I *have* found my true family.

*A beat, then she reaches for* CELESTE*'s hand.*

It's with Por and Celeste. Stand behind me, Celeste.

CELESTE: No, I'm right beside you.

*A huge climactic four-way battle. Drumming. Lights.*

*The two* SHEN DA PAIs *attack, both menacing, both equally evil.* TING TING *uses her ghost-fighting moves and* CELESTE *sings her powerful ghost song.*

*Both ghosts begin to waver and fall.*

*Finally the ghosts are both dissolved in a rush of light.*

TING TING: They're gone!
CELESTE: We dissolved them!

*They hug.*

Did you mean what you said before, about your true family?
TING TING: Yes. Por. And you.
CELESTE: Por Por! Where is she?

*They climb up out of the secret room.*

TING TING: [*finding a bag*] Por's ghost bag. I don't think she even had time to open it before he attacked. Look, [*holding it up*] here's her ming-shen mirror …
CELESTE: Por Por is somewhere here, I am sure of it.

*Beat.*

I can almost hear her … calling.
TING TING: It will take days to search this house.
CELESTE: Listen …

*Stepping forward, eyes closed, she listens, meditates.*

*Faint, creepy,* POR POR*'s voice from far away: 'Celeste', 'Ting Ting'.*

TING TING *doesn't know where the voice is coming from but* CELESTE *realises.*

The ming-shen mirror …

TING TING *looks at it and cries in alarm.*

TING TING: It's Por! Look! He trapped her inside! Por! She can't see us or hear us.
POR POR: [*faint voiceover*] Celeste! Ting Ting!
TING TING: Oh no … she'll be trapped forever.

*She begins to cry.*

Por was so good to me, so kind. She sacrificed so much …

CELESTE *takes the mirror carefully from her. Holds it up.*

CELESTE: Your tears … where they fell on the mirror, the glass is rippling …

TING TING: We need more tears?

CELESTE: It's not because of the tears, it's because the water is pure … we need more!

*She looks at* TING TING.

The lake … Por Por said the water was pure because it came from an underground spring.

TING TING: So all we need to do is wash the mirror in the lake … let's go.

*Reflected water sparkles about the stage.*

TING TING *and* CELESTE, *carrying the ming-shen mirror approach the lake. They dip it in the water. Then together they turn it over and tap on the back of the mirror.*

*A moment and then* POR POR *emerges, leaping up with a splash.*

CELESTE *and* TING TING *hug her.*

CELESTE *turns to the audience as* TING TING *and* POR POR *exit.*

## *14. TOMORROWS*

*The sound of water flowing.*

CELESTE: [*to the audience*] That night, I dream of our back garden at home. I hear water, flowing.

*The ghost song melody.*

And a song I recognise … And finally … I see her …

*A woman suddenly emerges nearby.*

Mama.

MAMA *carries a basket and kneels to one side, planting glowing shapes.*

Mama? What are you planting?

MAMA: [*smiling*] Come and see, Celeste.

CELESTE *walks towards her, carefully. Kneels beside her.*

CELESTE: They're so pretty. What are they?
MAMA: They are … tomorrows.

*The tomorrows begin to rise.*

CELESTE: You've planted … thousands! Thousands of tomorrows.
MAMA: They are all waiting. For you. Little Cloud.

MAMA *exits as* CELESTE *looks at the tomorrows.* CELESTE *doesn't see her leave.*

CELESTE: [*noticing she is gone*] Mama?

*The voice of* TING TING *pulls* CELESTE *out of the dream.*

TING TING: [*calling*] Celeste!

TING TING *and* POR POR *enter.*

*They are all on Mount Mystery, the mountain above the Isle of Clouds. Mist swirls about them.*

We're nearly there. Don't give up now!
CELESTE: [*taking the backpack*] I'm not giving up. I want to be first to see the view from the top of Mount Mystery!
POR POR: Be careful, both of you.

CELESTE *pauses at a spot on the path.*

CELESTE: Here. Here's the right place. Por Por. Ting Ting.

*She opens her backpack and takes out the little box she carried to China, unwrapping it from its cloth.*

*Behind her, we see the wooden ashes box projected on the large 'mother box' behind them.*

TING TING *and* POR POR *stand each side of* CELESTE, *supportive and loving.*

Mama … from up here, I see everything! The rice paddies and the roads. The bus full of frogs going over the stone bridge. The Isle of Clouds, the green canals and the black-tiled houses, I see Bao Mansion and the giant Fat Belly tree. I think I can even see Ling Feng on her boat of vegetables!
TING TING: Cabbages, lotus root …

CELESTE *joins in.*

TING TING and CELESTE: [*together*] Mushrooms and water spinach!
POR POR: [*gently*] And so many tomorrows.
CELESTE: Goodbye, Mama.

I love you.

Goodbye.

*Slowly, lovingly,* CELESTE *opens the box.*

*A breath and a flash of bright light.*

THE END